THE INNER CONSCIOUSNESS

A Course of Lessons on
The Inner Planes of the Mind,
Intuition, Instinct, Automatic Mentation and
Other Wonderful Phases of Mental Phenomena

By

WILLIAM WALKER ATKINSON

William Walker Atkinson
The Inner Consciousness
A Course of Lessons on The Inner Planes of the Mind,
Intuition, Instinct, Automatic Mentation and Other
Wonderful Phases of Mental Phenomena

First Published 1908
Advanced Thought Publishing Co.
Masonic Temple, Chicago, Ill.

Published 2024 by Jessica Dueber
31135 Hildesheim | Orleans - 22
Print edition and Kindle eBook by
Amazon Media EU S.à r.l., 5 Rue Plaetis,
L-2338 Luxembourg
ISBN 9798878743181

This book is an esoteric classic. The ideas and statements correspond to the knowledge and state of the art at the time it was written and should be read and understood in this context.

CONTENTS

I. INNER CONSCIOUSNESS

It was formerly taught in the schools that all of the Mind of an individual was comprised within the limits of ordinary Consciousness, but for many years this old idea has been gradually superceded by more advanced conceptions. Leibnitz was one of the first to advance the newer idea, and to promulgate the doctrine that there were mental energies and activities manifesting on a plane of mind outside of the field of ordinary consciousness. From his time psychologists have taught, more and more forcibly, that much of our mental work is performed outside of the ordinary field of consciousness. And, at the present time, the idea of an "Inner Consciousness" is generally accepted among psychologists.

Lewes says: "The teaching of most modern psychologists is that consciousness forms but a small item in the total of physical processes. Unconscious sensations, ideas and judgments are made to play a great part in their explanations. It is very certain that in every conscious volition — every act that is so characterized — the larger part of it is quite unconscious. It is equally certain that in every perception there are unconscious processes of reproduction and inference — there is a middle distance of subconsciousness, and a background of unconsciousness." And Sir William Hamilton states: "I do not hesitate to affirm that what we are conscious of is constructed out of what we are not conscious of — that our whole knowledge in fact is made up of the unknown and incognizable. The sphere of our consciousness is only a small circle in the centre of a far wider sphere of action and passion, of which we are only conscious through its effects." And Taine has said in connection with the same thought: "Mental events imperceptible to consciousness are far more numerous than the others, and of the world which makes up our being we only perceive the highest points — the lighted-up peaks of a continent whose lower levels remain in the shade. Beneath ordinary sensations are their components, that is to say, the elementary sensations, which must be combined into groups to reach our consiousness. Outside a little luminous circle lies a great large ring of twilight, and beyond this an indefinite night; but the events of this twilight and this night are as real as those within the luminous circle." To this, Maudsley adds his testimony, as follows: "Examine closely and without bias the ordinary mental operations of life, and you will surely discover that consciousness has not one-tenth part of the function therein which it is commonly assumed to have. In every conscious state there are at work conscious, sub-conscious and infra-conscious energies, the last as indispensable as the first."

It is now known that "Inner-Conscious" ideas, impressions and thoughts play a most important part in the thought-world of every individual. Beyond every outer-conscious action there may be found a vast inner-conscious background. It is held that of our entire mental processes, less than ten per cent are performed in the field of outer-consciousness. As a well known writer has so well expressed it: "Our self is greater than we know; it has peaks above and lowlands below the plateau of our conscious experience." Prof. Elmer Gates has forcibly put it: "At least ninety per cent of our mental life is sub-conscious. If you will analyze your mental operations you will find that conscious thinking is never a continuous line of consciousness, but a series of conscious data with great intervals of sub-consciousness. We sit and try to solve a problem and fail. We walk around, try again and fail. Suddenly an idea dawns that leads to a solution of the problem. The sub-conscious processes were at work. We do not volitionally create our own thinking. It takes place in us. We are more or less passive recipients. We cannot change the nature of a thought, or of a truth, but we can, as it were, guide the ship by a moving of the helm."

But, perhaps, the most beautiful expression of this underlying truth, is that of Sir Oliver Lodge, who says in his consideration of the subject: "Imagine an iceberg glorying in its crisp solidity, and sparkling pinnacles, resenting attention paid to its submerged self, or supporting region, or to the saline liquid out of which it arose, and into which in due course it will some day return. Or, reversing the metaphor, we may liken our present state to that of the hull of a ship submerged in a dim ocean among strange monsters, propelled in a blind manner through space; proud perhaps of accumulating many barnacles of decoration; only recognizing our destination by bumping against the dock-wall; and with no cognizance of the deck and cabins above us, or the spars and sails — no thought of the sextant, and the compass, and the captain — no perception of the look-out on the mast — of the distant horizon. With no vision of objects far ahead — dangers to be avoided — destinations to be reached — other ships to be spoken to by means other than by bodily contact — a region of sunshine and cloud, of space, or perception, and of intelligence utterly inaccessible below the water-line."

Dr. Schofield has cleverly and beautifully illustrated the idea in the following words: "Our conscious mind, as compared with the unconscious mind, has been likened to the visible spectrum of the sun's rays, as compared to the invisible part which stretches indefinitely on either side. We know now that the chief part of heat comes from the ultra-red rays that show no light; and the main part of the chemical changes in the vegetable world are the results of the ultra-violet rays at the other end of the spectrum, which are equally invisible to the eye, and are recognized only by their potent effects. Indeed as these invisible rays extend indefinitely on both sides of the visible spectrum, so we may say that the mind includes not only the visible or conscious part, and what we have termed the sub-conscious, that which lies below the red line, but also the supra-conscious mind that lies at the other end — all those regions of higher soul and spirit life, of which we are only at times vaguely conscious, but which always exist, and link us on to eternal verities, on the one side, as surely as the sub-conscious mind links us to the body on the other."

The late Frederic W. H. Myers, after years of careful study and research along the lines of the "out-of-consciousness" states, formulated a hypothesis of a "secondary self," or as he called it a "Subliminal Self," which "self" be held possessed certain powers which it exercised in a measure independent of the ordinary conscious "self." Perhaps the best explanation of his hypothesis has been stated by Mr. Myers, himself, in his book entitled "Human Personality." in which he states: "The idea of a threshold of consciousness — of a level above which sensation or thought must rise before it can enter into our conscious life — is a simple and familiar one. The word Subliminal — meaning 'beneath the threshold' — has already been used to define those sensations which are too feeble to be individually recognized. I propose to extend the meaning of the terra, so as to make it cover all that takes place beneath the ordinary threshold, or say, if preferred, the ordinary margin of consciousness — not only those faint stimulations, whose very faintness must keep them submerged, but much else which psychology as yet scarcely recognizes; sensations, thoughts, emotions, which may be strong definite, and independent, but which, by the original constitution of our being, seldom merge into that Supraliminal current of consciousness which we habitually identify with ourselves. Perceiving that these submerged thoughts and emotions possess the characteristics which we asociate with conscious life, I feel bound to speak of a Subliminal, or Ultra-marginal, Consciousness — a consciousness which we shall see, for instance, uttering or writing sentences quite as complex and coherent as the supraliminal consciousness could make them. Perceiving further that this conscious life beneath the threshold or beyond the margin seems to be no discontinuous or intermittent thing; that not only are these isolated subliminal processes comparable with isolated supraliminal processes (as when a problem is solved by some unknown procedure in a dream) but that there also is a continuous subliminal chain of memory (or more chains than one) involving just that kind of individual and persistent revival of old impressions and response to new ones, which we commonly call a Self — I find it permissible to speak of subliminal Selves, or more briefly a subliminal self. I do not indeed by using this term assume that there are two correlative and parallel selves existing always within each of us. Rather I mean by the Subliminal Self that part of the Self which is commonly subhrainal; and I conceive that there may be — not only many cooperations between these quasi-independent trains of thought — but also upheavals and alternations of personality of many kinds, so that what was once below the surface may for a time, or permanently, rise above it. And I conceive also that no Self of which we can here have cognizance is In reality more than a fragment of a larger self — revealed in a fashion at once shifting and limited through an organism not so framed as to afford it full manifestation."

We have given you the different views of these respective authorities not that we purpose adopting exclusively any of the various theories or hypotheses advanced, but merely that you may see that this question of an "Inner Consciousness" is not a mere vague theory of certain mystics and metaphysicians, but on the contrary is one that has attracted the earnest attention and consideration of scientific men and careful investigators along psychological lines. We shall have but very little to do with theories in this book — the Facts of the subject concern us more earnestly.

II. THE PLANES OF CONSCIOUSNESS

We have seen, in the preceding chapter, that many leading minds have recognized the existence, and phenomena of, certain Planes of Consciousness lying outside of (below or above) the ordinary plane or field of ordinary consciousness. Brushing aside as unimportant the various names and terms that have been aplied to these planes or fields of "inner consciousness," we easily find a common ground of agreement between all of the authorities. It is true that the subject has become somewhat clouded by the insistence of certain details of theory on the part of the several investigators, but they all practicaly agree upon the fundamental and basic facts and phenomena — and it is upon these basic and fundamental facts and phenomena that we shall rest our case as presented in this little book.

The student of psychology has heard much during the past decade regarding the many theories, some of them quite fantastic, designed to account for and explain the phenomena which science finds to exist and which it has classified as belonging to the inner-conscious plane of mental activity. Some of the theories advanced to account for the known facts and observed phenomena, have attracted to their support many followers, the respective schools holding animated and sometimes fierce content regarding the validity and superior qualities of their respective schools and their founders. But with these theories, and the schools which have been built up upon them, this work will have little to do or say. Enough for us is the fact of the existence of the phenomena, and the fact that there is certainly in manifestation an area of mental activity, which for reasons that we shall state we have called

"The Inner Consciousness." Recognizing the fact of the phenomena and accepting it as proven truth, we shall proceed to consider its manifestations, and apparent laws, and also the methods whereby one may use this mental activity to advantage. But we shall leave the theories to the theorists, and the discussions regarding the same to those who are fond of such exercises of the mind — for ourselves, we are tired of such things, and prefer to deal with observed facts, and the "how to get results" part of the question. We are apt to regard as a truth the observation of the writer who said: "Theories are but mighty soap-bubbles, with which the grown up children of science amuse themselves." And we also view with favor the lines of the poet in which he says:

"The nearer to the practical men keep—
The less they deal in vague and abstract things—
The less they deal in huge, mysterious words—
The mightier is their power.
The simple peasant who observes a truth,
And from the fact deduces principle,
Adds solid treasure to the public wealth.
The theorist who dreams a rainbow dream,
And calls hypothesis philosophy,
At best is but a paper financier
Who palms his specious promises for gold.
Facts are the basis of philosophy;
Philosophy the harmony of facts,
Seen in their right relation."

As a matter of fact, in order to account for the phenomena of the Inner Consciousness, it is not necessary to believe in, or assume, the hypothesis of any kind of a "dual-mind" at all. One mind may contain within itself suf&cient to account for the facts, without postulating a "two-mind" theory. One mind may contain within itself two, or many more than two, planes or fields of activity or consciousness, upon which and in which the varied mental phenomena may be manifested. In order to understand the phenomena of the Inner Consciousness, all that it is necessary for us to do is to start with the idea that in the mind of every person there are areas, fields, or planes of mental activity above and below the field, area, or plane that we know as "The Outer Consciousness." In other words, to assume (1) that there are basements, or cellars, vaults and sub-vaults of mind, below the level of the mental first floor in which we consider the results of our mental processes; and (2) is this true that also there are several mental stories above (as well as below) the one on which we do our "considering." And it is with these Several stories of mind — these planes or areas of mental activity — that we shall now have to do in this work.

As we have seen from the authorities quoted, the fields or areas of mind, outside of the circle of the Outer Consciousness, are many and varied. Careful investigators have divided the mental activities of these several planes or areas into two general classes, namely (1) those "below" the plane of outer consciousness, and which have the nature of automatic action; and (2) those "above" the plane of outer consciousness, and which have the nature of intuitive action, etc.

Some investigators have given to these two general planes or fields of mentation, the names of "the sub-conscious," and the "super-conscious," respectively — the term "sub" meaning "under, beneath, etc.," and the term "super" meaning "above, over, etc.," The trouble with this classification is that it places the "conscious mind," or that portion of our mentality the actions of which we may call "the outer," in the center of a scale, the extremes of which represent the higher and lower phases of "inner" mentation, respectively. This is not correct, for the so-called "conscious" mind is merely a "field of observation" before which passes the results of mental activity on the other planes, which when evolved pass into the field of consciousness, just as a star passes into the field of observation of a telescope, or a tiny object into the field of observation of the microscope, and is then perceived by the watching organ of vision. These objects passing into the "field of observation" of the outer consciousness, may come from the higher or lower planes of the Inner Mind. In fact the best observers know there can be no hard and fast line drawn between the activities and manifestations of the two respective groups of planes known as the "sub-conscious" and "super-conscious" minds. These activities shade into each other, and are like the degrees on a scale which are merely symbols which record the comparative and relative stages of manifestation of a thing, but which do not divide the thing into absolute divisions or classes.

In fact, the very best occult authorities inform us that there are very many degrees or "planes" of mental activity, higher and lower, outside of the field of observation oi the Outer Consciousness. On the lower planes of consciousness are to be found the consciousness of the various cells, and cell-groups, in our bodies, which constitute the "organ minds" which occultists know to exist. Then there are many planes of mentation concerned with directing the bodily activities. Then there are many planes of "thought" below the ordinary field of outer consciousness — and many planes of "awareness" and "knowing" above that of the ordinary intellectual operations of the average mind. These planes are merely the many degrees in the grand scale of Mind. We shall learn something of certain of them, as we proceed with these lessons.

Following the illustration of the "upper and lower stories, basements, cellars, sub-cellars, etc., we may say that it will help the student to think of the ordinary "Field of Observation" known as the Outer Consciousness of the Everyday Mind, as akin to the "Main Floor" of a warehouse, on which is received merchandise arriving from the outside business world ; and on which are started, packed and expressed the various goods, wares and merchandise reaching that department from the upper stories, basement, cellars and other storehouses of the mental warehouse and place of business, in pursuance to orders from "The Office". The Outer Consciousness, or Field of Observation and Consideration, is not a separate "Mind" as some claim, or the "Real Mind" as the masses of people consider it, but instead is merely a "department" of the whole mental business, in which the goods, stored articles, and manufactured goods from the other departments and workshops are sorted, selected, packed and expressed to the outer world. If you will fix this illustration in your mind, you will be able to easily assimilate and consider the facts to which we shall call your attention in the following lessons:

And, now, you see why we have adopted the terra "The Inner Consciousness" as applicable to both the higher and lower planes of the "extra-conscious" mental activities. The term "inner" means "further in; interior; internal; not outer, etc." The word "Consciousness" is one difficult to correctly define. In a general sense it means "mental awareness," but we have adhered to the closer meaning of the term which is used in the sense of "awareness of mental action and energy," or the quality by which Mind in activity is "aware" of its own activities. There can be no mental activity without consciousness on some plane, and the use of the word "unconscious" in connection with mental activity is an absurdity. There is consciousness, in some degree and on some plane, in everything, from the atom, and electron to the highest manifestation of super-human mind. And that which we call our "Outer Consciousness" is merely one of the many planes of the manifestation of the quality.

And, now let us proceed to our consideration of the phenomena and principles of manifestation of the "Inner Consciousness."

III. THE BASEMENTS OF THE MIND

In the lower planes of the Inner Consciousness are performed the various forms of mental activity which have to do with the building up, preservation, repairing, etc., of the physical body. Every cell has its share of mind, and every combination of cells into cell-groups and organs of the body, has its group or organ mind also. That which we call "Instinct" or "Nature" in a person or animal is a manifestation of Mind on some of the lower planes of the Inner Consciousness. And these lower planes are susceptible to suggestions or orders from other planes of mind, and will take on suggested ideas or conceptions, the result being that we are often made sick by ideas absorbed or suggested in this way; and we are likewise cured of physical ailments by similar methods, the suggested idea be placed on the proper plane by means of "auto-suggestion," "imparted ideas," and mental "treatments" of various kinds. Mind pervades every part of the physical body, and is always capable of being impressed by orders or suggestions coming from the more dominant portions of the mind of the individual. On some of the lower planes of the Inner Consciousness are to be found the seat and abode of the so-called "automatic" or "habit" actions of the mind. The Habit mind is made up of various things which have been placed there by the individual, which things were once performed in the field of consciousness, but which gradually became almost automatic by reason of experience, repetition, etc., until the performance of them passes from the held of consciousness down to some of the lower planes of the Inner Consciousness, thus becoming "second nature" and being likely to be repeated with little or no attention being bestowed by the conscious mind. You are familiar with this fact — all of you perform certain work almost automatically.

You run the sewing machine, typewriter, or play the piano almost automatically, and may be thinking of other things at the same moment. These tasks were originally performed only by an expenditure of much attention and effort on your part, but constant practice has enabled you to delegate the work to certain planes of your Inner Consciousness, until now they almost "work themselves," with a minimum of attention and concentration on your part. Some writers hold that no one really learns how to perform a task properly, until he or she is able to pass it down to this part of the mind, where it is performed almost automatically. Musicians and others are aware that their best work is performed by this part of their mentality, and that when, as occasionally happens, their conscious attention is directed to the work, there is a "slip up" and less perfect performance. The artist knows what it is to "lose himself" in his work and his greatest successes come at such times. Every writer knows this also, and the phenomena occurs in all manner and kinds of work. How many of us lose ourselves in "day-dreams" when performing our habitual tasks? How many of us seem to stand aside and watch ourselves work at tasks rendered familiar by habit.

We often cross the streets without paying conscious attention to our actions, and many of us have had the experience of "forgetting where we are going" and after a time finding ourselves brought up standing in front of the place from which we started. We put on our clothes in this way, the same arm going into the same sleeve, etc., without our thinking about the matter. If you will notice which arm you place in your coat the next time you dress, and then after taking off the coat again, try to insert the other arm first (reversing the regular order) you will be surprised to see how awkward you are, and how the "habit-mind" rebels at the change. The same is true of buttoning a collar — you always button on a certain tab first, and will find it most difficult to reverse the process.

We are in the habit of thinking of these things being "done by themselves" or as "doing themselves," but a moment's consideration will show you that nothing can manifest such activity except by means of mind of some kind and degree. The activity is the result of mental processes and direction, and without mind could not be performed. We may call it "automatic" or "mechanical" if we please, but it is really the result of mind — there is mind back of and in every "automatic" action of the individual. But being below the field of the outer consciousness, we do not recognize the mental operation. It is part of the phenomena of the lower planes of the Inner Consciousness.

And there are other planes of that wonderful region, in which certain "habits" are implanted, but which were not placed there by ourselves. We allude to the field of heriditary influences which have come down to us from those who lived before us throughout countless generations. There are planes of the Inner Consciousness filled with impressions, ideas, habits, emotions, feelings, desires and impulses which we have acquired by inheritance from the past. From the time of the cave men, and even further back, have come to us certain mental seeds and forces, which lie slumbering in the deep recesses of the lower planes of the Inner Consciousness. We are able to control and subdue, or else use, these latent impulses, by means of our higher mental faculties, but they are there just the same. As some writers have said, we have "the whole menagerie within us" — the tiger, the ape, the peacock, the donkey, the hyena, the goat, the sheep, the lion, and all the rest of the collection. We have come by these things honestly, and there is no reason to be ashamed of them — the shame consists only in turning these wild beasts loose into actions unworthy of our higher state gained through arduous evolution. As Luther Burbank has said: "Heredity means much, but what is heredity? Not some hideous ancestral specter, forever crossing the path of a human being. Heredity is simply the sum of all the effects of all the environments of all past generations on the responsive ever-moving life forces." And all of the effects of all the past environments of all past generations are registered, faintly or strongly on certain planes of our Inner Consciousness. An understanding of this fact will enable us to submit such tendencies when they occasionally poke their heads out from their dark caves in response to some familiar call which has roused them from their slumber — and an understanding will enable us to call upon the past within us for help and aid when we need the same to perform certain of the work of life. We have many things within us, which can and will manifest in outer consciousness when so called forth. We may use these things, or else allow them to use us, according to our degree of understanding and will power. But let us remind you always that there is nothing good enough to allow it to "use" you — use many things, but allow nothing to use you.

There are other planes of the Inner Consciousness in which rest the many suggestions placed there by your outer consciousness or that of others. You have a queer storehouse of acquired Suggestion, some good, some bad, and some neither or both. And from this storehouse comes the "habit-thought" of which such a large part of our mental processes are composed. In that storehouse are packed away countless impressions, ideas, opinions, prejudices, notions, likes and dislikes, and similar mental furniture. Much of this has been placed there by ourselves as the result of past thinking or half-thinking. And much has been placed there by the opinions, statements and suggestions of others, which we have admitted to our Inner Consciousness without due consideration and examination. As we shall see later on, this storehouse is an important part of our mental dwelling, and we should be careful just what we admit there. We shall also see that by means of Auto-Suggestion we may place there just what is likely to aid and help us in our lives, and that by the same means we may counteract the effect of many adverse and hurtful suggestions and "mental-habits" that we have allowed to find a home and storage room on these important planes of our minds. An understanding of these facts will be of the greatest importance and benefit to us.

On other planes of the Inner Consciousness are to be found the impressions and records comprising that which we know as "Memory." The Memory part of our mentality is like a vast collection of phonographic records upon which are registered the countless impressions that we have received during our life. Some of these records bear deep, clear and distinct impressions which when placed in the "Recollecting" machine send forth a clear reproduction of the original which produced the impression. Others contain impressions less clear — some bear very indistinct impressions, which are most difficult of reproduction. But there is this dfference between these memory records, and those of the phonograph. The phonographic records grow fainter and less perfect according to the frequency of their use, while the memory records register a still deeper and clear impression the oftener they are reproduced. If one dwells in memory upon certain past events, he will find that each reproduction gives out a clearer response. Of course, it is likewise true that one may mix outside facts and imaginary events with the real recollections, in some cases, so that in future reproductions the real and the false appear together. But this is merely another proof of the rule. One may (and many often do) add to a tale at each telling, until at last the re-told tale bears but little resemblance to the original — in so doing one mixes the new impressions with the old, on his mental phonographic records, and at the next reproduction both the original and the added points sound forth together. This is why some people "tell a lie so often that they actually believe it" — the repeated impressions upon the tablets of memory become deeper and clearer, and the notes of the false mix with those of the true. One should always endeavor to keep an honest collection of memory records, and be careful to avoid adding false impressions to the original ones.

It is astonishing that anyone at all familiar with the phenomena of Memory should doubt for a moment the existence of planes of consciousness beneath that of the ordinary outer consciousness. Every moment of our everyday life we are drawing upon these Inner Conscious Planes of Memory for the many things stored away there — far below the everyday outer consciousness. Not only do we draw upon these planes in this way, but in moments of intense stress — sudden danger — and other critical periods of life, these gates between these planes swing ajar and a flood of recollection pours out from them. It is related in numbers of instances that as a writer well expresses it: "The acts of a whole lifetime which are of consequence, and many that are not, will be flashed across the screen of memory with such lightning rapidity and with such distinctness as to seem like a vast panorama whose every detail is grasped by the mind in an instant of time. A noted high-bridge jumper, in describing hts feelings while making his famous leap from the Brooklyn bridge, stated that it seemed as if, during the few seconds required for his descent to the water beneath, there passed through his memory all the acts of his life, in their proper order — some of which had not appeared in his recollection for years, and which would have all his life remained dormant except for some extraordinary stimulus such as this. It is the almost universal experience of drowning persons who have been rescued at the last moment and resuscitated, that during the few moments just preceding the loss of consciousness, the memory suddenly grasps with a marvelous vigor the deeds of the life which seems about to end, and by some mysterious compelling intuition the sufferer is able and obliged to recognize at the same time, and more fully than ever before, the right or wrong of each particular act."

The following quotations will show you, at a glance, what an important part is played by this Inner Conscious faculty of Memory, in the domain of knowledge, in the opinion of eminent authorities:

"All knowledge is but remembrance." — Bacon.

"That which constitutes recollection or an act of memory is the present image which a past sensation has left in us, an image which seems to us the sensation itself." — Taine.

"Memory is a primary and fundamental faculty, without which none other can work; the cement, the bitumen, the matrix in which the other faculties are imbedded. Without it all life and thought were an unrelated succession." — Emerson.

"There is no faculty of the mind which can bring its energy into effect unless the memory be stored with ideas for it to look upon." — Burke.

"Every organ—indeed, every area and every element—of the nervous system has its own memory." — Ladd.

"Memory is the golden thread linking all the mental gifts and excellences together." — Hood.

"Memory is the cabinet of imagination, the treasury of reason, the registry of conscience, and the council-chamber of thought." — Basile.

"A man's real possession is his memory; in nothing else is he rich, in nothing else is he poor." — Alexander Smith.

"I would rather have a perfect recollection of all that I have thought and felt in a day or a week of high activity, than read all the books that have been published in a century." — Emerson.

And, after reading the above, remember that all of the records of Memory are stored away on the planes of the Inner Consciousness, the existence of which has been denied by the majority of people until very recently. In considering the marvelous phenomena of Memory, what thinking man can doubt that his Mind, and Self, are greater by far than the little, narrow field of outer consciousness, which is nothing by the eye-piece of his mental telescope, or microscope, before which pass in review the objects rising from, or super-imposed by, the planes of the Inner Consciousness?

IV. THE MENTAL STOREHOUSE

In the previous lessons we have stated that there are planes of the Inner Consciousness which resemble vast mental storehouses in which are placed the materials from which much of our thinking is composed. These thought-materials are brought by the porters and carriers of our mental warehouse into the field of consciousness, or thought-factory, where they are manufactured into the fabric of conscious thought and action. In those vast mental warehouses are much that we never placed there ourselves — the remnants of mental goods stored by countless ancestors, which are constantly being brought forward to be woven into the fabric of our thoughts. But, there are also vast quantities of material, good, bad and indifferent, placed there by ourselves, and it is these personal contributions to the storehouse which largely determine that thoughts and acts which result from what we call "our character" or our "nature." And this being the fact, is it not of the greatest importance that we should be careful just what kind of material we place in these great mental warehouses and storage chambers? Our present thoughts and actions — our characters, in fact, are largely the result of our past thoughts and mental attitude. And the thoughts, actions and character of each of you, in the future, will be largely the result of the mental material which you are now placing in these storage rooms of your mind. This is not "preaching" or "moralizing," but is merely the calling of your attention to facts and truths known to, and admitted by, all students of psychology.

We are today largely the result of what we have thought, or what we have allowed to impress us in the past. Our Mental

Attitude, together with the kind of suggestions that we have allowed to impress us in the past, determines to a great extent our "character" and "self" of today. When we think, we do not manufacture the thought-fabric out of the thin air, or sunlight, or out of "nothing" as many seem to suppose. Each bit of wonderful fabric of thought and action is the result of the weaving of the mental material that we have accumulated in the past and stored away in some of the storage rooms of the Inner Consciousness. This surely is plain enough to everyone who will give the matter a moment's thought, and yet how few really have realized the truth and still fewer are those who have learned to act upon this principle. If we were building a house, store or any other building, how careful we would be to see that none but the best materials were delivered to the builders in whose hands the erection of the property was placed. How carefully each item of inaterial would be inspected. If we were in the manufacturing business, and wished to turn out goods of fine quality, how careful we would be regarding the grade of the material to be used. Our buyer would exercise his sldll, and the inspector would look over each consignment as it arrived, rejecting all imperfect and unsatisfactory material. And yet, how careless we are regarding our thoughts, moods, mental attitudes, and auto-suggestions that we place among the material to be used in our mental building and manufacturing in the days to come. Is it not time to call a halt on these careless and almost criminal methods, and adopt a sane, scientific plane of thought-life?

The Mental Attitude of a man is represented by the character of thoughts which he allows to "take a hold on him." If he allows every despondent, negative, hurtful thought to obtain lodgment in his mind, his mental attitude will gradually become in harmony with such thoughts, and he will be laying away a fresh stock of negative thoughts each day. which will surely be woven into the mental-fabric he turns out on some future day. Can you doubt this, when you know of the effects of certain mental "habits" of manifestation? And what are these habits, but the using of the thought-material of the past? How much harder is it for a man whose mind is full of these negative thought-materials to present a bold, confident, courageous front in the battles of life? His every instinct and habit of thought is against it. It is so much easier to droop the shoulders, and fold the hands, and say "what's the use?" in such a case — because all the mental material is of that dark grey, negative hue — all the material is of that rotten, worthless quality. But if, in the past you have cultivated the habit of refusing to admit the negative thoughts and suggestions — have thrown them out on the scrap-pile, and have stored away nothing but the bright, cheerful, courageous and positive thoughts and suggestions — then when you begin to build or weave you will surely produce the best kind of thought and action. You cannot help it, for you are working with the best materials, and with your mental machine adjusted to the proper gauge.

All this is far more than "jollying" or "cheering-up talk" — it is a statement of psychological fact which if once thoroughly understood by the masses of people, would make this old world of ours over into a much brighter and cheerful place. An understanding of these principles will make you over mentally, if you will but act upon your new knowledge. There is no "secret process" connected with this work — all that is necessary for you to do, is to Will that henceforth you will allow no negative, depressing or undesirable thought take lodgment in your mind, but will on the contrary keep steadily at work replacing the undesirable things in your mind with desirable material. When a negative thought comes into your field of consciousness, dismiss it with the thought "there is another bit of that mental truck that I stored away — away with it to the scrap-pile." And lose no opportunity of thinking the bright, optimistic, positive, desirable thoughts, and storing them away. And when you can put one of these thoughts into action, by all means do so, for by so doing you have added a large share to the right kind of material in your mental storehouse.

Do not let the thought of the past thought-foolishness worry you or discourage you. Think of the comparison, made by a well-known writer who compared the mind to a bowl of muddy water, into which a clear stream of fresh water was pouring. Anyone will see that the fresh water will gradually clear the entire body of water, until the muddy substances are not discernible. So pour in the kind of thoughts you desire, and thus render clear the muddiness that has been your bane for so long. Another writer has compared the matter to a dark room — if you wish to drive away the darkness, just open the shutters and admit the light, and lo! the darkness has disappeared. And this last illustration is true according to the old occult teachings which held that a "positive" thought always tended to neutralize and transmute a "negative" one — in fact that a positive thought bad sufficient potency and force to neutralize many negative thoughts. This being the case, by will-power, and perseverance, you may change the nature of your mental-materials stored away in the storerooms of the Inner Consciousness, including the inherited orteS, and thus render yourself practically a new person in character and nature, within a reasonable time.

The Ego is the real master, and not the slave of environment that so many seem to think it is. It is true that when the Ego lies dormant and passive, the personality is indeed made up of the inherited ideas and feelings; the suggested thoughts and ideas; and the acquired ideas and tendencies picked up during our life. But let the Ego once rouse itself and put into operation its own weapon — the Will — then it is enabled to master environment, and to cast out the rubbish stored away from the past, replacing it with bright, fresh, good strong mental material from which the thoughts and actions of the future will be manufactured. The Ego can re-make one's "character," for it is the Master of the Mental Warehouse. Dismiss your careless and incompetent mental assistants, which have allowed this accumulation of mental rubbish. Take charge yourself — You, the Ego — and assert your Mastery. Inspect and pick out your own mental material, that nothing but the best quality of thought and action may be produced!

V. "MAKING-OVER" ONESELF

One of the most interesting phases of the science of using the Inner Consciousness, is that which may be called "making-over" oneself. That is, the application of psychological laws in the direction of rebuilding certain of the Inner Conscious planes, or rather in replacing the mental material stored there by the more desirable material. This process has been aptly called "Character Building," which indeed it is, for the character is largely dependent upon what is contained in the Inner Consciousness, and whatever affects the latter affects the Character.

The word "Character" itself, is derived from a Greek word meaning "to engrave"; to "cut in"; and some of the authorities state that the Greek word was derived from some older language and was first used by the ancient makers of bricks to indicate the personal trade mark marked by each upon the bricks manufactured by himself, each maker having his own trade mark. And the word has gradually grown in meaning until today we use it in the sense of "the peculiar quality, or sum of qualities, by which a person or thing is distinguished from others." (Webster.) This latter-day use of the term is interesting when one is able to trace it from its original usage, showing the idea that was in the minds of those who have gone before us, i. e., that this thing that we call "character" was something impressed or engraved upon a man's mental substance. To the majority of persons character is something that belongs to a person, by some unchangeable natural law, and which cannot be altered or improved. To the experienced psychologist, however, character is a plastic thing, which is modified by the character of one's thoughts and mental attitude, and which may therefore be improved, changed or altered at will.

Psychology, taking cognizance of the planes of Inner Consciousness, and understanding the truth of the fact that character is the fabric manufactured from the material stored away on those planes, now teaches that by placing the proper materials in the storage rooms we may cause the character to be manufactured in accordance with the quality thereof. In short, that one may practically "make-over" oneself by placing the right kind of "raw material" in the mind. This is true in the case of training children and others, but is equally true in Self Training or Character Building.

To those who may think that in speaking of the planes of the Inner ConscEousness, we are postulating a shadowy, intangible, "mind," independent of the brain, we would say that this is not correct. We regard the brain as the organ of the mind, in its Inner Conscious manifestations as well as in its outer-conscious ones. The brain is composed of an enormous number of cells, composed of "plasm" or elementary living matter, some authorities estimating the number of the brain-cells at about 500,000.000 to 3,000,000,000, the number depending upon the mental activity of the person. Beside the number of brain-cells in active use, there are always great reserve forces of cells awaiting a sudden call. In addition to this, it is beheved that the brain will "grow" additional cells in cases of need, so that the mind capacity of the individual is almost limitless. A class of brain-cells actively used will manifest a tendency to spring into activity almost automatically, at the slightest need, while those remaining unused will become almost atrophied, and are called into action slowly and clumsily. It therefore follows that the cells which are constantly used will exert a more marked influence upon the character of the individual than will those become atrophied by disuse. Therefore, if one will but use a set of cells actively, they will manifest strongly in his everyday life and character.

To develop traits of character in oneself, that we consider desirable but lacking, we should endeavor to think and act as often as possible along the lines that we wish to develop. Just as we exercise the muscle that we wish to bring up to a higher degree of efficiency, so should we exercise the faculties of the mind that we wish to increase in power and strength. And at the same time, we should avoid developing the opposite set of faculties. And if we wish to rid ourself of, or restrain an objectionable set of faculties, we should actively use and thus develop the opposite set, so as to counteract the undesirable ones. As Halleck says: "By restraining the expression of an emotion we can frequently throttle it; by inducing an expression we can often cause its allied emotion." Prof. James says : "Refuse to express a passion, and it dies. Count ten before venting your anger, and its occasion seems ridiculous. Whistling to keep up courage is no mere figure of speech. On the other hand, sit all day in a moping posture, sigh, and reply to everything with a dismal voice, and your melancholy lingers. There is no more valuable precept in moral education than this, as all of us who have experienced it know: If we wish to conquer undesirable emotional tendencies in ourselves we must assiduously, and in the first instance cold-bloodedly, go through the outward movements of those contrary dispositions which we wish to cultivate. Smooth the brow, brighten the eye, contract the dorsal rather than the ventral aspect of the frame, and speak in a major key, pass the genial compliment and your heart must indeed be frigid if it docs not gradually thaw."

To sum up the matter of "Making-over" Oneself, we may say that the whole secret consists in filling up the particular storage-room having to do with the desired faculty, and its opposite, with thoughts, actions, desires, manifestations, etc., of the desired thing. Think of the thing; act it out so far as possible; desire it ardently; picture it out to yourself as much as possible; in short, keep its mental image before you as clearly and as persistently as possible. It is an old occult maxim that "we grow to be like the thing that we keep constantly in our mind" — and if you will but keep that axiom in your mind, you will work out the problem for yourself.

The secret underlying much of the phenomena called "occult" is the creation of what is known as a "Mental Image," and which is really a mental pattern or mould from which we wish to materialize character in ourself or others. This Mental Pattern or Mould serves as a "model" around which is built the actual mental manifestation. And the clearer and stronger we build this Mental Image, the better and stronger results do we materialize. Keep in mind constantly the idea of the thing you wish to be, and you will unconsciously grow toward being just that thing. This is a well established psychological law, and is not a mere airy fancy of some writer's imagination. You can see it evidenced in the life of yourself and those around you. Everyone unconsciously inclines toward the shape and form of the Mental Image that they carry around with them. And, this being so — that we grow to resemble our Ideals — should we not be careful to use the right kind of mental patterns or moulds? Our manifested character depends upon the mental patterns created by ourselves, either by our own will and according to our own judgment, or else, unconsciously, from the suggestions or will of others.

Aristotle wrote that of every object of thought there must be in the mind some form, phantasm, or Species; that things sensible are perceived and remembered by means of sensible phantasms, and things intelligible by intelligible phantasms; and that these phantasms have the fonn of the object without the matter, as the impression of a seal upon wax has the form of a seal without its matter. The student of modem psychology may see, at a glance, just what Aristotle meant — the Mental Image which moulded or served as a pattern for the thought which would spring from the Inner Consciousness. Kay says: "It is as serving to guide and direct our various activities that mental images derive their chief value and importance. In anything that we purpose or intend to do we must first of all have an idea or image of it in the mind, and the more clear and correct the image, the more accurately and efficiently will the purpose be carried out. We cannot exert an act of volition without having in mind an idea or image of what we will to effect." The same writer also says: "Clearness and accuracy of image is only to be obtained by repeatedly having it in mind or by repeated action of the faculty. Each repeated act of any of the faculties renders the mental images of it more clear and accurate than the preceding, and in proportion to the clearness and accuracy of the image will the act itself be performed easily, readily, skillfully."

And, now, all this that we have said on the subject means simply that you CAN "make over" yourself, to be that which you desire to be, by means of determined and persistent desire and will. By filling up the storage-rooms of the proper plane of the Inner Consciousness with the "Ideals" and "Ideas" which you desire to materialize in your own character and self, you will find that you will gradually begin to grow like the Mental Image that you have placed there. Your thoughts, actions, feelings and emotions will gradually be found to be reshaping themselves to fit in to the pattern or mould which you have set before them. The material which has been placed in the storage-rooms will be brought forth by the silent mental workers and, being placed into the mental machinery will be manufactured into thoughts, moods, feelings, emotions, actions and outward manifestations of the grade and quality indicated by the materials which you have supplied. You cannot make silk from cotton, nor broadcloth from shoddy. Unless you furnish the proper materials you cannot expect the finished product to be as you desire. You are making character and "self" every day — but it depends upon the material furnished just what that character or self shall be. An understanding of the Inner Conscious workings of the mind gives you the only key to the mystery of character and self— then why not act upon it?

VI. "AUTOMATIC THINKING"

The advanced writers on the subject of psychology have given us many examples of the workings of the mind on the planes of what some have aptly called "Automatic Thinking," We feel that it will be well to quote a few cases to illustrate this phase of the subject.

There are many instances stated of persons who had been earnestly endeavoring to solve certain problems and questions, but who had been compelled to lay aside the matters as incapable of solution at the time. In a number of such cases it is related that while thinking of something entirely foreign to the subject the long sought answer would suddenly flash into the tield of consciousness, of course without any conscious effort on the part of the person. A well known writer, in giving an instance of the kind which had happened to him personally, states that when the answer came to him in this way he trembled as if in the presence of another being who had communicated the secret to him in a mysterious manner. Nearly every person has had the experience of trying to remember a name, word, date, or similar thing, without success, and then after dismissing the matter from the mind have had the missing idea or word suddenly flashed from the Inner Consciousness into the field of the ordinary consciousness. Some part of the Inner Consciousness was at work trying to supply the demand, and when it found it it presented it to the person.

Another well known writer gives several cases of what he calls "unconscious rumination," in which the mind worked silently, and below the field of the ordinary consciousness, after the person had read works relating to new subjects, or presenting new points of view essentially opposed to previously conceived opinions and views. He states that in his own experience, he found that after days, weeks, or even months, he would awaken to a realization that his old opinions were entirely rearranged, and new ones had taken their place. Some have called this process "sub-conscious mental digestion and assimilation." and indeed the process is akin to the work of the physical organism in digesting and assimilating material nourishment.

Sir William Hamilton is stated to have discovered an important mathematical principle while walking one day in the Dublin Observatory. He stated that upon the occasion he "felt the galvanic circle of thought close," and the sparks that fell from the mental process were the fundamental mathematical relations of his problem, which as all students know now forms an important law in mathematics.

Thompson the psychologist has written as follows on this subject: "At times I have felt a feeling of uselessness of all voluntary effort, and also that the matter was working itself clear in my mind. It had many times seemed to me that I was really a passive instrument in the hands of a person not myself. In view of having to wait for the results of these unconscious processes, I have proved the habit of getting together material in advance, and then leaving the mass to digest itself until I am ready to write about it. I delayed for a month the writing of my book 'System of Psychology,' but continued reading the authorities. I would not try to think about the book. I would watch with interest the people passing the windows. One evening while reading the paper, the substance o£ the missing part of the book flashed upon my mind, and I began to write. This is only a sample of such experiences."

Berthelot, the eminent French chemist who founded the present system of Synthetic Chemistry, has said that the experiments leading to his remarkable discoveries in that branch of science were seldom the result of carefully followed lines of conscious thought or pure reasoning processes, but, instead, came of themselves, from a clear sky, so to speak. Mozart, the great composer, once said: "I cannot really say that I can account for my compositions. My ideas flow, and I cannot say whence or how they come. I do not hear in my imagination the parts successively, but I hear them, as it were, all at once. The rest is merely an attempt to reproduce what I have heard." In addition to the experience above mentioned. Dr. Thompson has stated that: "In writing my work I have been unable to arrange my knowledge of a subject for days and weeks, until I experienced a clearing up of my mind, when I took my pen and unhesitatingly wrote the result. I have best accomplished this by leading the mind away as far as possible from the subject upon which I was writing."

Oliver Wendell Holmes has said: "The automatic flow of thought is often singularly favored by the fact of listening to a weak continuous discourse, with just enough ideas in it to keep the mind busy. The induced current of thought is often rapid and brilliant in inverse ratio to the force of the inducing current." Wundt has also said, on this subject: "The unconscious logical processes are carried on with a certainty and regularity which would be impossible where there exists the possibility of error. Our mind is so happily designed that it prepares for us the most important foundations of cognition, whilst we have not the slightest apprehension of the *modus operandi*. The unconscious soul, like a benevolent stranger, works and makes provisions for our benefit, pouring only the mature fruits into our laps." An English writer has stated: "Intimations reach our consciousness from unconsciousness, that the mind is ready to work, is fresh, is full of ideas. The grounds of our judgment are often knowledge so remote from consciousness that we cannot bring them to view. The human mind includes an unconscious part; unconscious events occurring in that part are proximate causes of consciousness; the greater part of human intuitional action is an effect of an unconscious cause — the truth of these propositions is so deducible from ordinary mental events, and is so near the surface, that the failure of deduction to forestall induction in the discerning of it may well excite wonder. Our behavior is influenced by unconscious assumptions respecting our own social and intellectual rank, and that of the one we are addressing. In company we unconsciously assume a bearing quite different from that of the home circle. After being raised to a higher rank the whole behavior subtly and unconsciously changes in accordance with it. Commenting on the above, another writer adds: "This is also the case in a minor degree with different styles and qualities of dress and different environments. Quite unconsciously we change our behavior, carriage, and style, to suit the circumstances."

Jensen has written: "When we reflect on anything with the # whole force of the mind, we may fall into a state of entire unconsciousness, in which we not only forget the outer world, but also know nothing at all of ourselves and the thoughts passing within us after a time. We then suddenly awake as from a dream, and usually at the same moment the result of our meditations appears as distinctly in consciousness without our knowing how we reached it." Another writer has said: "It is inexplicable how premises which lie below consciousness can sustain conclusions in consciousness; how the mind can wittingly take up a mental movement at an advanced stage, having missed its primary steps." Some psychologists, Hamilton and others, have made a comparison likening the action of the mental processes to that of a row of billiard balls, of which one is struck and the impetus transmitted throughout the whole row, the result being that the last ball actually moves, the others remaining in their places. The last ball represents the plane of ordinary outer consciousness, the other balls representing the various stages of the action of the Inner Consciousness. Lewes, the psychologist, commenting on the above conception, adds: "Something like this, Hamilton says, seems often to occur in a train of thought, one idea immediately suggesting another into consciousness, this suggestion passing through one or more ideas which do not themselves rise into consciousness. This point, that we are not conscious of the formation of groups, but only of a formed group, may throw light on the existence of unconscious judgments, unconscious reasonings, and unconscious registrations of experience."

In connection with these processes of the mind, on the planes below those of the outer consciousness, many writers have noted the discomfort and uneasiness preceding this birth into consciousness of the ideas developed on the unconscious planes. Maudsley says regarding this: "It is surprising how uncomfortable a person may be made by the obscure idea of something which he ought to have said or done, and which he cannot for the life of him remember. There is an effort of the lost idea to get into consciousness, which is relieved directly the idea bursts into consciousness." Oliver Wendell Holmes says: "There are thoughts that never emerge into consciousness, and which yet make their influence felt among the perceptive currents, just as the unseen planets sway the movements of the known ones." He adds: "I was told of a business man in Boston who had given up thinking of an important question as too much for him. But he continued so uneasy in his brain that he feared he was threatened with palsy. After some hours the natural solution of the question came to him, worked out, as he believed, in that troubled interval."

The above experiences are common to the race, and nearly everyone who reads the above lines will at once recognize the occurrences as familiar in his or her own mental experience.

Among the many interesting cases related to illustrate the principle of "automatic thing," or "unconscious rumination," that of the famous mathematical prodigy, Zerah Colbum, is perhaps one of the most striking. This individual possessed a remarkable faculty of "automatically working out the most difficult mathematical problems." It is related of him, that while yet a child of seven years of age, and while he was without any previous knowledge of the common rules of arithmetic, he was still able by some intuitive, Inner Conscious faculty, to solve the most difficult mathematical problems without the aid of figures, pencils or paper — by some Inner Conscious system of Mental Arithmetic. At that early age, he was able in this way to immediately give the number of minutes and seconds in any given period of time, and to tell the exact product arising from the multiplication of any number consisting of two, three or four figures, by any other number consisting of a like number of figures. The records of his times give many wonderful instances of his strange power, from which we quote the following, as an illustration:

"At a meeting of his friends, which was held for the purpose of concerting the best methods of promoting the views of the father, this child undertook and completely succeeded in raising the number 8 progressively up to the sixteenth power. And in naming the last result, viz., 381,474,976,710,656, he was right in every figure. He was then tried as to other numbers consisting of one figure, all of which he raised as high as the tenth power, with so much facility and despatch that the person appointed to take down the results was obliged to enjoin him not to be so rapid. He was asked the square root of 106,929; and before the number could be written down, he immediately answered, 327. He was then required to name the cube root of 268,336,135; and witli equal facility and promptness he replied, 645. Various other questions of a similar nature, respecting the roots and powers of very high numbers, were proposed, to alt of which he answered in a similar manner. One of the gentlemen asked him how many minutes there were in forty-eight years, and before the question could be written down he replied, 25,228,800; and then instantly added that the number of seconds in the same period was 1,513.728.000. He persistently declared that he did not know how the answers came into his mind. Moreover, he was entirely ignorant of the common rules of arithmetic, and could not perform upon paper a simple sum in multiplication or division. In the extraction of roots, and in mentioning the factors of high numbers, he gave the answers either immediately, or in a very few seconds; whereas it requires, according to the ordinary method of calculation, very difficult and laborious work, and much time." A most peculiar sequel was noted in this case, for as the child was educated to perform mathematical calculations according to rule, and in the ordinary way, his wonderful power deteriorated, and in the end he was no more than the ordinary well-drilled child, so far as the branch of mathematics was concerned.

The instance of Blind Tom is also an illustration of "automatic thinking," for this poor, blind creature — but little above idiocy so far as ordinary knowledge was concerned — possessed something in his Inner Consciousness that enabled him to play any piece that he had ever heard, even years before, with perfect reproduction of detail; and to also improvise wonderful strains, and harmonies. Something was at work on the Inner Conscious planes of this poor black man's mind — as if to show to a doubting and materialistic world the possibilities of the human mind and soul in its hidden phases.

In view of the above instances, and many other similar ones, can you doubt that there are planes of mental action, outside of the ordinary consciousness, on which in some marvelous manner mental work can be, and is, done? Even if the experience of nearly everyone did not furnish proof, surely the recorded cases should place the matter above the plane of doubt. And yet, so strong is the spirit of Doubt, that many will say: "Yes, but — !"

VII. INNER-CONSCIOUS HELPERS

Many of you have heard the old fairy-tales and bits of folk-lore relating to the kindly "brownies" or "good fairies", who, feeling affection for, and gratitude toward, some poor tailor or cobbler who had befriended them, would come at night, when the workman and his family were asleep, and taking up the unfinished work that had been left on the table or bench, would work diligently at it so that when the morning's sun roused the worker from his slumbers he would find his unfinished task completed. The little hands of the brownies would have fashioned the leather into shoes, then stitched and pegged them; the cloth would be cut and made into garments; the pieces of wood would be made into boxes, chests, furniture, chairs, etc. The rough material had been prepared by the workman during the day; the brownies would "do the rest." But what has all this to do with the Inner Consciousness, you may ask. Just this — that in the Inner Consciousness of each of us there are forces which act much the same as would countless tiny mental brownies or helpers who are anxious and willing to assist us in our mental work, if we will but have confidence and trust in them. No, this is no fairytale; it is by a psychological truth expressed in the terms of the old fairy tale.

By reference to Lessons III and VI, you will see mentioned many instances of the work of these Inner Conscious Helpers. In Lesson VI, especially, you will notice several instances in which well-known authorities testified to the fact that there was a marked manifestation of "automatic thinking" or "unconscious rumination," by means of which problems which had proved unsolvable by the conscious mind had been gradually worked out by the Inner

Consciousness, and the results then duly presented to the field of outer consciousness. The facts are well known to psychologists and many investigators have learned to use the law to their own benefit.

The process of calling into service these Inner Conscious Helpers is similar to that by which we constantly employ the Memory to recall some forgotten fact or name. We find that we cannot recollect the desired fact, date or name, and instead of racking our brains with an increased effort, we (if we have learned the secret) pass on the matter to the Inner Consciousness, with a silent command "remember this name for me," and then go on with our ordinary work. After a few minutes — or it may be hours — all of a sudden, pop! will come the missing name or fact before us — flashed from the planes of the Inner Consciousness, by the help of the kindly workers or "brownies" of those planes. The experience is so common that we have ceased to wonder at it, and yet it is a wonderful manifestation of the Inner Conscious workings of the mind. Stop and think a moment, and you will see that this missing word does not present itself accidentally or "just because". There are mental processes at work for your benefit, and when they have worked out the problem for you they gleefully push it up from their plane on to the plane of the outer consciousness where you may use it.

We know of no better way of illustrating the matter than by this fanciful figure of the "mental brownies," in connection with the illustration of the "Mental Storehouse." If you would learn to take advantage of the work of the Inner Conscious Brownies, form a mental picture of the Mental Storehouses on the several planes of the Inner Consciousness, in which are stored all sorts of knowledge that you have placed there during your lifetime, as well as the impressions that you have had passed on to you from the past — whether that past be the lives of ancestors, or past lives of yourself, take your choice regarding this. The information stored away has often been placed in the storage rooms without any regard to systematic storing, or arrangement, and when you wish to find something that has been stored away a long time ago, the exact place being forgotten, you are compelled to call to your assistance the little brownies of the mind, which you do by the silent command of "recollect this for me." These brownies are the same little chaps that you charge with the task of waiting you up at four o'clock tomorrow morning when you must catch your train — and they obey you well. The same little fellows will also flash into your consciousness the report, "I have an engagement at two o'clock with Jones" — and looking up at your clock you can see that it is just a quarter before the hour of your engagement.

Well, if you will examine carefully into a subject which you wish to master, and will pass along the results of your observations to these Inner Conscious brownies, you will find that they will work the raw materials into shape for you in time. They will arrange, analyze, systematize, collate and arrange in consecutive order the various details of information which you have passed on to them, and will add thereto the various articles of similar information that they will find stored away in the various recesses of your memory. In this way they will group together various scattered bits of knowledge that you have forgotten. And, right here, let us say to you that you never absolutely lose anything that you have placed in your mind. You may be unable to remember to recollect certain things, but they are not lost — sometime later some associative connection will be made with some other fact, and lo! the missing idea will be found fitted nicely into its place in the larger idea — the work of our little brownies. Read the examples given in other lessons — they can be reproduced by you or anyone who will cultivate the "knack" of it. Remember Thompson's statement that: "In view of having to wait for the results of these unronscious processes, I have proved the habit of getting together material in advance, and then leaving the mass to digest itself until I am ready to write about it." This Inner Conscious digestion is the work of our little mental brownies.

There are many ways of setting the brownies to work. Nearly everyone has had some experience, more or less, in the matter, although often it is done almost unconsciously and without intent or knowledge. Perhaps the best way for the average person — or rather, for the majority of persons — is to get as clear an idea of what you really want to know as possible — as clear an idea or mental image of the question you want answered — and then, after rolling it around in your mind, giving it a high degree of voluntary attention, then, we say, pass it on to the Inner Conscious planes, with the mental command, "Attend to this for me — work out the answer, and then report to me" or a similar order. This order may be made silently, or aloud if you wish — the forming of the words seems to give force to the order. Speak to the Inner Conscious workers just as you would to people in your employ, firmly but kindly. And, then — and this is an important point — you must accompany the order with an Earnest Expectation that your Will will be carried out. The clearer your belief the better will be the result. A doubt will interfere somewhat. The writer of this book once said: "Earnest Desire — Confident Expectation — and Firm Demand — these form the Triple Key of Occult Attainment."

And so it is, in this case as in many others. Talk up to your Inner Consciousness, and firmly command it to do your work — but also Earnestly Desire its accomplishment — and above all. Confidently Expect the desired answer. And then forget all about the matter — throw it off of your conscious mind, and attend to other tasks. And then in due time the answer will be forthcoming, and will flash before your consciousness — perhaps not until the very minute that you must decide upon the matter, or need the information. You may give your brownies orders to report by such and such a time, if you wish — just as you do when you tell them to awaken you for your train, or to remind you of your appointment.

VIII. "FORETHOUGHT"

The late Charles Godfrey Leland, a well-known writer, and investigator along psychological lines, devoted several of the last years of his long life (he lived to be nearly eighty years of age) to an investigation of the operation of the Will along the general lines of Inner Consciousness. He, of course, did not use the term "Inner Consciousness," but he recognized the existence of its planes of mental manifestation, and his ideas fit very nicely into the subject-matter and ideas advanced in this book, particularly so far as concerns the actual employment of the power possible to those v?ho understand the subject. In connection with the idea ol "automatic thinking," which we have described in the two preceding chapters, under the head of "automatic thinking," and "Inner conscious helpers," he uses the word "Forethought" (first employed in a similar connection by Horace Fletcher), He uses the term "Forethought" in the same sense that we use the term "mental command" to the figurative brownies of the Inner Conscious planes. We think it advisable to quote liberally from him in this lesson and the one immediately following, in which latter the "Leland Method" is described. Mr. Leland's ideas are so practical, and bo readily understood by the average person, that you will do well to read closely these quotations. Mr. Leland says; "Forethought is strong thought, and the point from which all projects must proceed. As I understand it, it is a kind of impulse or projection of Will into the coming work, I may here illustrate this with a curious fact in physics. If the reader wished to ring a door-bell so as to produce as much sound as possible, he would probably pull it as far back as he could, and then let it go. But if he would, in letting it go, simply give it a tap with his forefinger, he would actually redouble the sound. Or, to shoot an arrow as far as possible, it is not enough to merely draw the bow to its utmost span or tension. If, just as it goes, you will give the bow a quick push, though the effort be trifling, the arrow will fly almost as far again as it would have done without it. Or, if, as is well known, in wielding a very sharp sabre, we make the draw-cut, that is, if to the blow or chop, as with an axe, we also add a certain slight pull, simultaneously, we can cut through a silk handkerchief or a sheep. Forethought is the tap on the bell; the push on the bow; the draw on the sabre. It is the deliberate but yet rapid action of the mind when before falling to sleep or dismissing thought, we bid the mind to subsequently respond. It is more than merely thinking what we are to do; it is the bidding or ordering the Self to fulfill a task before willing it.

"Forethought, in the senses employed or implied, as here described means much more than mere previous consideration or reflection, which may be very feeble. It is, in fact, constructive, which implies active thought. Therefore, as the active principle in mental work. I regard it as a kind of self-impulse, or that minor part in the division of the force employed which sets the major into action. Now, if we really understand this, and can succeed in employing Forethought as the preparation for, and impulse to, Auto-Suggestion, we shall greatly aid the success of the latter, because the former insures attention and interest. Forethought may be brief, but it should always be energetic. By cultivating it we acquire the enviable talent of those men who take in everything at a glance, and act promptly, like Napoleon. This power is universally believed to be entirely innate, or a gift; but it can be induced or developed in all minds in proportion to the will by practice.

"Be it observed that as the experimenter progresses in the development of will by Auto-Suggestion, he can gradually lay aside the latter, or all processes, especially if he work to such an end, anticipating it. Then he simply acts by clear will and strength and Forethought constitutes all his stock-in-trade, process or aid. He preconceives and wills energetically at once, and by practice and repetition Forethought becomes a marvellous help on all occasions and emergencies. To make it avail the one who frequently practices Auto- Suggestion, at first with, and then without sleep, will inevitably find ere long that to facilitate his work, or to succeed, he must first write, as it were, or plan a preface, synopsis, or epitome of his proposed work, to start it and combine with it a resolve or decree that it must be done, the latter being the tap on the bell-knob. Now the habit of composing the plan as perfectly, yet as succinctly as possible, daily or nightly, combined with the energetic impulse to send it off, will ere long give the student a conception of what I mean by Forethought, which by description I cannot. And when grown familiar and really mastered, it will give to its possessor a power to think and act promptly in all the emergencies of life, in a greatly increased degree.

"All men of great natural strength of mind, gifted with the will to do and dare, the beings of action and genius, act directly, and are like athletes who lift a tree by the simple exertion of the muscles. He who achieves his aim by self culture, training, or Autosuggestion, is like one who raises the weight by means of a lever, and if he practice it often enough he may in the end become as strong as the other. Such a man is like the hero in one of Mayne Keid's novels, of whom it is said: 'His aim with the rifle is infallible, and it would seem as if the ball obeyed his Will. There must be a kind of Directing Principle in his mind, independent of strength of nerve and sight. He and one other are the only men in whom I have observed this singular power.' This means simply the exercise tn a second, as it were, of the tap on the bell-knob, or the projection of the will into the proposed shot, and which may be aplied to any act.

"Mind and especially Forethought, or reflection, combined in one effort with will and energy, enters into all acts, though often unsuspected, for it is a kind of reflex action or cerebration. Thus I once discovered to my astonishment in a gymnasium that the extremely mechanical action of putting up a heavy weight from the ground to the shoulder, and from the shoulder to the full reach of the arm above the head, became much easier after a little practice, although my muscles had not grown, nor my strength increased during the time. And I found that whatever the exertion be, there was always a trick or knack, however indescribable, by means of which the man with a brain could surpass the dolt at anything, though the latter were his equal in strength. But It sometimes happens that the trick can be taught and improved upon. And it is in all cases Forethought, even the lifting of weights or the willing on the morrow to write a poem.

"This acting or working of the two thoughts at once (the thought of just what you want, and the thought that you succeed) may be difficult for some readers to understand. It may be formulated thus: 'I wish to remember tomorrow at four o'clock to visit my bookseller — bookseller's — four o'clock — four o'clock.' But with practice the two become as one conception. When the object of a state of mind, as, for instance, calmness all day long, is obtained, even partially, the operator (who must of course do all to help himself to keep calm, should he remember his wish) will begin to believe in himself sincerely, or in the power of his will to compel a certain state of mind. This won all may be won, by continued reflection and perseverance. It is the great step gained, the alphabet learned, by which the mind may pass to boundless power. This process of Auto-Suggestion, and trusting to the effect of ordinary sleep, is well adapted to producing desired states of mind, including those manifesting in future action.

"Forethought can be of vast practical use in cases where confidence is required. Many a young clergyman and lawyer has been literally frightened out of a career, and many an actor ruined for want of a very little knowledge, and in this I speak from personal experience. Let the aspirant who is to appear in public, or pass an examination, and is alarmed, base his Forethought on such ideas as this, that he would not be afraid to repeat his speech to one or two persons — why then should he fear a hundred persons? There are some who can repeat this idea to themselves, till it takes hold strongly, and they rise almost feeling contempt for all in court, as did a lady in St Louis, who felt so relieved when a witness at not feeling frightened, that she bade the judge and jury to cease looking at her in that impudent way, "It will be useless for any person to take up this method as a trifling pastime or to attempt Auto-Suggestion and development of Will with as little earnestness as one would give to a game of cards; for in such half-hearted effort time will be lost and nothing come of it. Unless centered upon with the most serious resolve to persevere, and make greater effort and more earnestly at each step, it had better be left alone. All who persevere with calm determination cannot fail crc long to gain a certain success, and this achieved, the second step is much easier.

However, there are many people who after doing all in their power to get to the gold or diamond mines hasten away even when in the full tide of success, because they are fickle. And such people are more wearisome and greater foes to real Science than the utterly indifferent or the ignorant. This will not have been written in vain should it induce the reader to reflect on what is implied by patient repetition or perseverance, and what an incredible and varied power that man acquires who masters it.

"There are many cases in which the reader may ask me whether this method may be employed, to which I am compelled to answer that I have had no experience in such cases. But I may add, in such cases, that as regards the method, I am like the Scotch clergyman, who, being asked by a wealthy man if he thought the gift of a thousand pounds to the Kirk would save the donor's soul, replied: 'I'm na prepairet to preceesly answer thot question— but
I wad vara warmly advise ye to try it.'"

IX. THE "LELAND METHOD"

Mr. Leland, whose remarks on Forethought we gave you in the preceding lesson, paid much attention to a method of using the "Inner Consciousness" which is generally known as "The Leland Method." Other writers, before and after Mr. Leland's work, have considered this phase of the subject, but Mr. Leland deserves much credit for having brought the matter before the attention of a large number of people in so practical a manner, and in so forcible a style. We herewith give you the gist of his "method," in his own words, culled from his works on the subject. Mr. Leland begins by stating that for a number of years he had given much attention, time, study and reflection to the subject of the methods of impressing the Inner Conscious planes of the mind with Auto-Suggestions (Forethoughts; Mental Commands; Orders to the Brownies. etc.,) given immediately before one would sink to sleep at night. He then goes on to say:

"All mental or cerebral faculties can by direct scientific treatment be influenced to what would have once been regarded as miraculous action, and which is even yet very little known or considered. In the development of this theory, and as confirmed by much practical and personal experience, the Will can by very easy processes of training, or by aid of Auto-Suggestion, be strengthened to any extent, and states of mind soon induced, which can be made by practice habitual. Thus, a man. by a very simple experiment a few times repeated — an experiment which I clearly describe and which has been tested and verified beyond all denial — can cause himself to remain during the following day in a perfectly calm or cheerful state of mind; and this condition may, by means of repetition and practice, be raised or varied to other states or conditions of a far more active or intelligent description. Thus, for illustration, I may say that within my own experience, I have by this process succeeded since my seventieth year in working all day far more assiduously, and without any sense of weariness or distaste for labor than I ever did at any previous period of my life. And the reader need only try the extremely easy experiment, as I have described it, to satisfy himself that he can do the same, that he can continue it with growing strength ad infinitum."

Mr Leland then goes on to point out to the reader the effects of Auto-Suggestion, which are known to all students of psychology. He says: "Then it came to my mind that since Auto-Suggestion was possible, that if I would resolve to work all the next day; that is, apply my self to literary or artistic labor without once feeling fatigue, and succeed, it would be a marvelous thing for a man of my age. And so it befell that by making an easy beginning I brought it to pass to perfection. What I mean by an easy beginning is not to will or resolve too vehemently, but to simply and very gently, yet assiduously, impress the idea upon the mind so as to fall asleep while thinking of it as a thing to be. My next step was to will that I should, all the next day, be free from any nervous or mental worry, or preserve a hopeful, calm, or well-balanced state of mind. This led to many minute and extremely curious experiments and observations. That the imperturbable or calm state of mind promptly set in was undentable, but it often behaved like the Angel in H. G. Wells' novel, 'The Wonderful Visit', as if somewhat frightened at, or of, with, or by its new abode, and no wonder, for it was indeed a novel guest, and the goblins of 'Worry and Tease, Fidget and Fear' who had hitherto been allowed to riot about and come and go at their own sweet wills, were ill-pleased at being made to keep quiet by this new lady of the manor. I had my lapses, but withal I was simply astonished to find how, by perseverance, habitual calm not only grew upon me, but how decidedly it increased. And far beyond perseverance in labor, or the inducing a calmer and habitually restful state of mind, was the Awakening of the Will, which I found aa interesting as any novel or drama, or series of active adventures which I have ever read or experienced."

Then Mr. Leland proceeds to impart to his readers his "discovery," or "method," as follows: "And this is the discovery: Resolve before going to sleep that if there be anything whatever for you to do which requires Will or Resolution, be it to undertake repulsive or hard work or duty; to face a disagreeable person; to last; or make a speech; to say "No!" to anything; in short, to keep up to the mark or make any kind of effort that you WILL DO IT— as calmly and unthinkingly as may be. Do not desire to do it sternly or forcibly, or in spite of obstacles — but simply and coolly make up your mind to DO IT — and it will much more likely be done. And it is absolutely true that if persevered in, this willing yourself to will by easy impulse unto impulse given, will lead to marvelous and most satisfactory results."

Mr. Leland then gives the following words of caution to those undertaking the practice of his method: "There is one thing of which the young or over sanguine or heedless should be warned. Do not expect from this method, or anything else in this life, prompt perfection or the maximum of success. You may pre-determine to be cheerful, but if you are very susceptible to bad weather, and the day should be dismal, or you should hear of the death of a friend, or a great disaster of any kind, some depression of spirits will likely ensue. On the other hand, note well that forming habit by frequent repetition of willing yourself to equanimity and cheerfulness, and also to the banishing of repulsive images when they come, will infallibly result in a very much happier state of mind. As soon as you actually begin to realize that you are acquiring such control, remember that is the golden hour — and redouble your efforts. I trust that I have thus far in a few words explained to the reader the rationale of a system of mental discipline based on Will, and how by a very easy process the latter may be gradually awakened. Everyone would like to have a strong, vigorous Will, and there is a library of books or sermons in some form, exhorting the weak to awaken and fortify their wills or characters, but all represent it as a hard and vigorous process, akin to storm and stress, battle and victory, and none really tell how to go about it. I have indeed only indicated that it is by Auto-Suggestion that the first steps are taken.

"If we will that a certain idea shall recur to us on the following, or any other day, and if we bring the mind to bear upon it just before falling asleep, it may be forgotten when we awake, but it will recur to us when the time comes. That is what almost everybody has proved, that if we resolve to awake at a certain hour we generally do so; if not the first time, after a few experiments, apropos of which I would remark that no one should ever expect full success from any first experiment. Just by the same process as that which enables us to awake at a given hour, and simply by substituting other ideas for that of time, we can acquire the ability to bring upon ourselves pre-determined or desired states of mind. This is Auto-Suggestion, or deferred determination, be it with or without sleep. It becomes more certain in its results with every new experiment or trial. The great factor in the whole is perseverance or repetition. By faith we can remove mountains, by perseverance we can carry them away, and the two amount to precisely the same thing.

"And here be it noted what, I believe, no writer has ever before observed, that as perseverance depends upon renewed forethought and reflection, so by continued practice and thought, in Auto-Suggestion, the one practicing begins to find before long that his conscious will is acting more vigorously in his waking hours, and that he can dispense with the sleeping process. For, in fact, when we once find that our will is really beginning to obey us and inspire courage and indifference where we were once timid, there is no end to the confidence and power which may ensue. Now this is absolutely true. A man may will certain things ere he fall asleep. This willing should not be intense, as the old magnetizers taught; it ought rather to be like a quiet, firm desire or familiarization with what we want, often gently repeated until we fall asleep in it. So the seeker wills or wishes that he shall, during all of the next day, feel strong and vigorous, hopeful, energetic, cheerful, bold, or calm, or peaceful, as he may desire. And the result will be obtained just in proportion to the degree in which the command or desire has impressed the Sub-Conscious Mind, or sunk into it.

"But, as I have said: Do not expect that all of this will result from a first trial. It may even be that those who succeed very promptly will be more likely to give out in the end than those who work up from small beginnings. The first step may very well be that of merely selecting some particular object, and calmly and gently, yet determinedly directing the mind to it, to be recalled at a certain hour. Repeat the experiment; if successful add to it something else. Violent effort is unadvisable; yet mere repetition without thought is time lost. Think, while willing, what it is that you really do want; and, above all, if you can, think with a certainty and feeling that the idea will surely recur to you.

"To recapitulate and make all clear we will suppose that the reader desires during the following day to be in a calm, self-possessed or peaceful state of mind. Therefore at night, after retiring, let him first completely consider what he wants and means to acquire. This is the Forethought, and it should be as thorough as possible. Having done this, will or declare that what you want shall come to pass on waking, and repeating this and thinking on it, fall asleep. This is all. Do not wish for two things at once, or, not until your mind shall have become familiar with the process. As you feel your power strengthen with success, you may will yourself to do whatever you desire.

"It may have struck the reader as an almost awful or at least a very wonderful idea, that Man has within himself, if he did but know it, tremendous powers or transcendental faculties of which he has really never had any conception. One reason why such bold thought has been subdued is that he always felt according to tradition, the existence of superior supernatural beings, by whose power and patronage he has been effectively restrained or kept under. It may seem a bold thing to say that it did not occur to any philosopher through the ages, that Man, resolute, noble and free, might Will himself into a stage of mind defying devils and phantasms, or that amid the infinite possibilities of human nature, there was the faculty of assuming the Indifference habitual to animals when not alarmed. Our method renders potent and grand, pleasing or practically useful, to all who practice it, a faculty which has the great advantage that it may enter into all the relations or acts of life; will give to everyone something to do, something to occupy his mind, even in itself, and if we have other occupations."

The student will recognize in the "Leland Method" the same principles of Auto-Suggestion, of Self-Command. that we have referred to in other lessons, together with the principle of the "Mental Helpers" already spoken of. But he will also notice the stress and importance that Mr. Leland attaches to the idea of giving the Command or Auto-Suggestion just before one goes to sleep. This idea, in fact, forms the key-note of the Leland Method, and Mr. Leland's ideas have attracted much attention by reason thereof, notwithstanding that the idea of Suggestion before sleep has been referred to and written upon by other writers, before and since the date of Mr. Leland's work. But. inasmuch as the latter brought out this phase of the subject so clearly, it is but just that any presentation of the general subject contain a liberal reference to his work, theories and ideas, and full credit for the same.

There is a good psychological reason underlying the fact that Mental Commands given to one's own mind just before sleep should prove so efficacious. The reason lies in the fact that sleep is a state induced by nature not only for the purpose of resting the physical body and enabling the reparative and recuperative processes to work to the best advantage — important as is this work, there is still another purpose behind the phenomena of sleep. During sleep there is a mental work going on, as well as a physical. The tiny worker of the mind (to follow the figurative illustration already used by us) — the "brownies" of the mind, do much of their work during the time of sleep. The period of sleep is the time of "great doings" on some of the planes of the Inner Consciousness. Then is to be found the performance of the work of mental assimilation, analysis, collation, combining, adjusting, storing-away, arranging, etc., of the material gathered by the outer consciousness, through its sense organs and reasoning faculties during the waking hours just past. The workers of the mind gather up the material roughly stored at the end of the day, and store it away systematically, each impression according to its kind, and according to the law of association, so that when one starts on a certain subject he will find arranged in order all that he knows concerning that subject — the process is like the arrangement of books in a large modern reference library, so that anyone familiar with the system may go from one book to another until he has acquainted himself with all the library contains concerning that particular subject.

But this is not all. During the day the conscious mind has made numerous demands for certain information — answers — work — solutions, etc., more or less unconsciously, and the little workers of the mind take this their first chance to do this work, now that the outer consciousness is asleep and not bothering them with demands for the performance of the numerous tasks of the day that demand immediate attention. They gather together the scattered material, and like the brownies work up the material into perfected articles, so that the next day the individual is surprised to find how his mind has worked out many matters for him while he was asleep. These little brownies "work while you sleep," as the current slang expresses it.

And so now you see the value of the "Leland Method." Just before going to sleep you formulate a definite demand upon the brownies, and then dismiss the subject from your outer consciousness. Then while you are asleep the desired task is accomplished — the missing link to the chain of knowledge is forged and adjusted into place — the puzzling problem is solved — the perplexing riddle is answered. But you must always remember that after you have said to your Inner Consciousness, "Attend to this for me while I sleep", you must then positively dismiss the matter from your outer consciousness, just as a great executive dismisses a matter when he gives it over to a tried and trusted assistant. Until you do this the Inner Consciousness cannot do its work properly. Always remember this in connection with this phase of the subject. It is highly important.

X. INTUITION AND BEYOND

Just as there are mental planes which the investigator naturally classifies as "below" the ordinary planes of consciousness— the instinctive plane; the physical-function plane; the habitplane, and even the plane on which the so-called "automatic thinking," etc., manifests — so are there many planes which one naturally thinks of as "above" the ordinary plane. As we have said, not only are there the basements and sub-cellars beneath the floor of the packing and shipping department of the mind, but also many "upper stories" above that floor. Upon these upper floors of the mind rest those things which the world calls Genius; Inspiration; Intuition; Spiritual Power; and other names denoting higher faculties of the mind.

Kay says: "It is in the ultra-conscious region of the mind that all its highest operations are carried on. It is here that genius works." Carlyle said: "Shakespeare's intellect is what I call an unconscious intellect; there is more virtue in it than he himself is aware of. The latest generations of men will find new meanings in Shakespeare, new elucidations of their own human being." Goethe said: "I prefer that the principle from which, and through which, I work shall be hidden from me." Ferrier says: "The sublimest works of intelligence are quite possible, and may be easily conceived to be executed, without any consciousness of them on the part of the apparent and immediate agent." Holmes says: "The creating and informing spirit which is within us and not of us, is recognized everywhere in real life. It comes to us as a voice that will be heard; it tells us what we must believe; it frames our sentences and we wonder at this visitor who chooses our brain as his dwelling place." Schofield says: "The supra-conscious mind lies at the other end — all those regions of higher soul and spirit life, of which we are only at times vaguely conscious, but which always exist, and link us on to eternal verities, on the one side, as surely as the sub-conscious mind links us to the body on the other."

Schofield also says: "The mind, indeed, reaches all the way, and while on the one hand it is inspired by the Almighty, on the other it energizes the body, all whose purposive life it originates. We may call the supra-conscious mind the sphere of the body life, the sub-conscious mind the sphere of the body hfe, and the conscious mind the middle region where both meet." Schofield also says: "The Spirit of God is said to dwell in believers, and yet, as we have seen. His presence is not the subject of direct consciousness. We would include, therefore, in the supra-conscious, all such spiritual ideas, together with conscience — the voice of God, as Max Muller calls it — which is surely a half-conscious faculty. Moreover the supra-conscious, like the sub-conscious, is, as we have said, best apprehended when the conscious mind is not active. Visions, meditations, prayers, and even dreams have been undoubtedly occasions of spiritual revelations, and many instances may be adduced as illustrations of the workings of the Spirit apart from the action of reason or mind. The truth apparently is that the mind as a whole is an unconscious state, by that its middle registers, excluding the highest spiritual and lowest physical manifestations, are fitfully illuminated in varying degrees by consciousness; and that it is to this illuminated part of the dial that the word "mind", which rightly appertains to the whole, has been limited." And as Emerson has said: "Trust the instinct to the end, though you can render no reason. It shall ripen into truth, and you shall know why you believe."

In the region of the higher planes of the Inner Consciousness are to be found that wonderful aspect or phase of mind which we call "Intuition," which Webster defines as: "Direct apprehension or cognition: immediate knowledge, as in perception or consciousness involving no reasoning process." Intuition is a most difficult thing to describe, but yet nearly everyone understands just what is meant by the term. It is a higher form of that which we know as "Instinct," the difference being chiefly that Instinct belongs to the phenomena of the "below" conscious planes, and has to do chiefly with that which concerns the physical body and well-being — while Intuition belongs to the "above" conscious planes and has to do with the higher part of the nature of the individual. Instinct sends its messages "up" to the Intellect, while Intuition sends its messages "down" to the Intellect. Many of the highest form of pleasurable things come from the region of Intuition. Art, Music, Poetry; the love of the Beautiful and the Good; the higher forms of love; intuitive perception of truth; all these come from above — from the region of Intuition.

Genius also comes from that enchanted region. All great writers, poets, painters, musicians, actors, and artists of all kinds and modes of expression have received their "Inspiration" from these higher regions of the mind. All great artists, working through the various mediums of expression noted above, have felt that their best work was rather the result of the labor of some higher power, rather than of their own "every-day self." The testimony on this point is overwhelming. And, strange to say, the work that impresses itself most strongly upon the public, is just this kind of work which left upon the mind of the worker the impression that it came "from above" — was the result of "inspiration." The Greeks, recognizing the wonderful phenomena emanating from this part of the mind, were wont to call it the work of the "daemon," or "spirit," which, friendly to the artist, would attach itself to him and "inspire" his work. Plutarch wrote that Timarchus saw in a vision the spirits which were partly attached to human bodies, and partly over and above them, shining luminously over their heads. In the vision, he was informed by the oracle that the part of the spirit which was immersed in the body was called the "soul," while the outer or unimmersed portion was called the "daemon" or "spirit." The oracle also stated that every man had his daemon, whom he was bound to obey; those who implicitly follow that guidance are the prophetic souls, the favorites of the gods. This idea of the "daemon" was a favorite one with Socrates, and even Goethe was evidently impressed with the idea, for he speaks of the daemon as a power higher than the will, and which inspired certain natures with miraculous energy. Of course these ideas were merely the attempts of the thinkers of those days attempting to account for and explain the phenomena which was apparent to all. There is no necessity for postulating the existence of these "daemons" or "spirits" to account for the phenomena of Intuition and Genius. The "daemon" is merely the operation of the mind of each of us on its higher planes. We have it all within us — that Something Within which seems almost like a protecting and guiding entity.

In this connection we quote the following from a well-known work: "The advanced occultist knows that in the higher regions of the mind are locked up intuitive perceptions of all truth, and that he who can gain access to these regions will know everything intuitively, and as a matter of clear sight, without reasoning or explanation. The race has not as yet reached the heights of Intuition — it is just beginning to climb the foothills. But it is moving in the right direction. It will be well for us if we will open ourselves to the higher inner guidance, and be willing to be 'led by the Spirit.' This is a far different thing from being led by an outside intelligence, which may, or may not, be qualified to lead. But the Spirit within each of us has our interests at heart, and is desirous of our own best good, and is not only ready but willing to take us by the hand and lead us on. The Higher Self is doing the best it can for our development and welfare, but is hampered by its confining sheaths. And, alas, many of us glory in these sheaths and consider them the highest part of ourselves. Do not be afraid to let the light of the Spirit pierce through these confining sheaths and dissolve them. The Intuition, however, is not the Spirit, but is one of its channels of communication to us. There are other and still higher planes of mind, but the Intuition is the one next above the Intellect in the line of unfoldment, and we should open ourselves to its influence and welcome its gradual unfoldment and manifestation within ourselves."

There are indeed planes of the Inner Consciousness above that which we know as Intuition, but the consideration of these would take us beyond the scope of this little work and on to the great field of what has been called "Spiritual Consciousness," and which is as yet practically undeveloped in the majority of the race. In this great field is also included that plane of consciousness which has been called "Cosmic Consciousness," in which certain highly developed individuals have been able to penetrate, and thus realize in actual consciousness that Oneness of Life and the Unity in the Universe. But, as we have said, this belongs to an entirely different phase of the general subject from that which we are considering in this work. The purpose of this little work is chiefly to point out to the students the various fields of consciousness common to the whole race, and which may be developed by any individual, together with certain suggestions concerning this work of development and use. Therefore, we must pass by with a mere mention those exacted planes of consciousness which have been penetrated only by certain highly developed individuals. In fact, these higher planes can scarcely be called "mental planes" at all — they belong to that part of man's nature which is more properly designated "spiritual." The possibilities before any man and every man along the lines pointed out in this work axe sufBciently great for the majority of individuals, and the development and use of these various mental planes will "keep them busy" for a long time to come. And when finally they are ready for further progress, the way will open itself out for them, and the book or the teacher will be found ready to give the needed instruction.

While the phase of the subject of Inner Consciousness, known as Spiritual Consciousing — that spiritual "knowing" by means of which one is able to see through and behind the things of the material plane — belongs to another branch of occult science, and can scarcely be touched up in this work, still it would not be just to the reader for us to fail to call his attention to the higher planes of his own being, which are unfolding into conscious realization as he advances in spiritual unfoldment and attainment.

All of us have recognized that "Something Within" which comes to our aid in times of doubt, distress and trouble. Many of us have considered this "Something" to be outside of themselves, but it is really a higher part pf the soul awakened into greater activity by the needs of the individual. This *Something Within* is always alert and awake to our interests, and tries to send us a warning word or a restraining hand, but alas! we brush these loving admonitions aside as "mere imagination," "absurd notions," etc., and refuse to accept the message coming from the higher planes of our own being. Not only in times of danger does the *Something Within* send us its messages — it tries to help us even in the little affairs of every-day life. Did you never feel an earnest desire for some information of a certain kind and, after failing to find it, later be led to some book shelf in a store or in a public library and, picking up a book at random, find either the information you wish or else a reference to some other book containing the information? Many have had these experiences — perhaps you are one of the number. Have you never had the experience of being "led" to a person or place in order to gain certain information or advantages? Have you never been "led" apparently in the opposite direction from where you thought a desired something might be found, only to find later that in that opposite direction was the thing you desired? Have you never been conscious of the little mental "nudges" in this direction, or the little restraining "pull-back" drawing you away from certain things — afterwards to find that the suggestion of the *Something Within* had been actually right, whether you followed it or not ?

These things are not mere imaginings, but are the manifestations of that Something which is the higher part of ourselves, always striving and trying to guide us aright. The old tales about "Conscience" were founded on true scientific facts – each of us has that which folks have called a "Conscience," trying to "steer the way true" for each of us. This *Conscience* or *Something Within* is not the "goody-goody" thing that has been taught, but instead is a watchful

Something, knowing better and seeing farther than can we in our outer consciousness, and endeavoring to steer us aright. Do not reject these things as "played-out relics of out-grown creeds." but recognize them for what they are.

Learn to recognize the pressure of the "Unseen Hand" — welcome it when it comes, and bid it welcome. Do not shake it from your shoulder as an alien thing, simply because you fail to understand it and its laws. Trust to its well-meaning and kindliness. It is not an outside thing — it is a part of your very self. It will manifest according to your faith in and expectation its presence. It is striving to unfold further and further into your conscious life, and you may aid it by bidding it welcome and treating it as a part of yourself instead of as an alien. It is Yourself who is speaking — so do not shut the door of your mind to it.

Let the light within you send its rays into your outer consciousness, that it may illumine and make plain the way that your feet must tread. And step out boldly upon the place illumined for your footsteps without fear and with confidence. If you understand these things clearly you will know what good old Newman meant when he wrote the beautiful lines:

"Lead, kindly Light, amid the encircling gloom,
Lead thou me on.
The night is dark, and I am far from home;
Lead thou me on.
Keep thou my feet; I do not ask to see
The distant scene; one step enough for me;
Lead thou me on."

Printed in Great Britain
by Amazon

42804605R00046